BOTANICAL CHARACTERISTICS	3
PHYSICAL APPEARANCE	3
DIFFERENT SPECIES AND VARIETIES	5
POPULARITY AS A GARDEN PLANT	7
LANDSCAPE USES	8
CULTURAL SIGNIFICANCE	10
CULTIVATION AND PROPAGATION	13
IDEAL GROWING CONDITIONS AND SOIL REQUIREMENTS	16
IMPACT OF CLIMATE CHANGE	19
CONSERVATION EFFORTS	20
SEASONAL CARE AND MAINTENANCE	22
COMMON PESTS AND DISEASES	25
POTENTIAL BENEFITS FOR PETS AND ANIMALS	28
DANGER TO KIDS AND HOME PETS	30
STAGES OF GROWTH AND DEVELOPMENT: FROM SEED TO MATURE PLANT	32
ROLE IN LANDSCAPING AND GARDEN DESIGN	35
DIFFERENT USES IN GARDENING	38
PRESERVING AND DRYING PEONY PLANTS FOR DECORATIVE PURPOSES	41
HYBRIDIZATION AND BREEDING TECHNIQUES FOR CREATING NEW PLANT VARIETIES	44
ROLE OF PEONY IN TRADITIONAL MEDICINAL PRACTICES AND HERBAL REMEDIES	47
CHALLENGES AND COMMON MISTAKES IN GROWING PEONY PLANTS	50

- CHALLENGES IN CONSERVATION AND PRESERVATION OF PEONY PLANTS 53
- SYMBOLISM OF PEONY IN WEDDINGS AND CELEBRATIONS 56
- ROLE OF PEONY PLANTS IN BIODIVERSITY CONSERVATION AND CONTRIBUTION TO LOCAL ECOSYSTEMS 59
- TRADITIONAL USES OF PEONY IN BEAUTY AND COSMETICS 62
- CULINARY USES OF PEONY IN FOOD AND BEVERAGES ... 65
- USE OF PEONY PLANTS IN CRAFTS 67
- MYTHS AND LEGENDS SURROUNDING PEONY IN DIFFERENT CULTURES 70
- METHODS OF USING PEONY IN AROMATHERAPY 73
- CHEMICAL COMPOSITION AND MEDICINAL PROPERTIES OF PEONY 76
- THERAPEUTIC USES OF PEONY FOR HUMANS 79
- ROLE OF PEONY IN MODERN CULTURE 82
- WAYS TO ENJOY AND APPRECIATE PEONY 85
- CONCLUSION: EMBRACING THE BEAUTY OF PEONY 88
- CONCLUSION: EMBRACE THE DELIGHTFUL CHARM OF PANSIES 90

PEONY

BOTANICAL CHARACTERISTICS

Peony is a flowering plant belonging to the genus Paeonia, which is part of the family Paeoniaceae. It is a herbaceous perennial plant that typically grows to a height of 1 to 3 feet (30 to 90 centimeters). Peonies are known for their large, showy flowers and are widely cultivated for their ornamental value.

PHYSICAL APPEARANCE

The physical appearance of peonies can vary depending on the species and cultivar, but they generally have the following characteristics:

FLOWERS:

Peony flowers are large and fragrant, measuring 3 to 6 inches (8 to 15 centimeters) in diameter. They have numerous petals arranged in multiple layers, giving them a lush and full appearance. The petals come in a wide range of colors, including white, pink, red, and yellow. Some peony varieties also exhibit bi-color or multi-color patterns.

LEAVES:

The leaves of peonies are dark green in color and are composed of several leaflets. The leaflets are oval or lance-shaped and have a glossy texture. The foliage is typically dense and provides an attractive backdrop to the flowers.

STEMS:

The stems of peonies are sturdy and erect, providing support to the flowers. They are usually green or reddish-brown in color and have a smooth texture.

ROOTS:

Peonies have a thick and fleshy root system known as a tuberous root. The roots are typically brown in color and have numerous smaller roots branching off from them.

Overall, peonies are known for their stunning flowers and lush foliage, making them popular choices in gardens and floral arrangements.

PEONY

DIFFERENT SPECIES AND VARIETIES

1. PAEONIA LACTIFLORA

Paeonia lactiflora, commonly known as the Chinese peony or common garden peony, is one of the most popular species of peony. It features large, fragrant flowers in various shades of pink, red, and white. This species has numerous cultivars, including 'Sarah Bernhardt' with double pink flowers and 'Bowl of Beauty' with pink outer petals and a center of creamy yellow.

2. PAEONIA OFFICINALIS

Paeonia officinalis, also known as the common peony or European peony, is a species native to Europe. It has single or double flowers in shades of pink, red, and white. One notable cultivar is 'Rubra Plena' with double deep red flowers that are highly fragrant.

3. PAEONIA SUFFRUTICOSA

Paeonia suffruticosa, commonly called the tree peony, is a woody shrub-like peony species native to China. It produces large, stunning flowers in various colors, including white, pink, purple, and yellow. The 'High

Noon' variety is known for its bright yellow flowers, while 'Shimadaijin' features striking deep red petals.

4. PAEONIA TENUIFOLIA

Paeonia tenuifolia, also known as the fern-leaf peony, is a unique species characterized by its finely dissected, fern-like foliage. The flowers are typically red and have a distinctive center of yellow stamens. 'Flamingo' is a popular cultivar with double red flowers and dark purple foliage.

5. INTERSECTIONAL HYBRIDS

Intersectional hybrids, also called Itoh peonies, are a cross between herbaceous and tree peonies. They combine the best traits of both parents, producing large and vibrant flowers on sturdy stems. Varieties such as 'Bartzella' display yellow double flowers, while 'Cora Louise' showcases pink and cream petals.

These are just a few examples of the many species and varieties of peonies available. Each has its own unique characteristics, making peonies a diverse and captivating group of plants.

PEONY

POPULARITY AS A GARDEN PLANT

Peonies are highly popular as garden plants and are widely cultivated for their beauty and versatility. Here are some reasons for their popularity:

1. STUNNING FLOWERS:

Peonies are known for their large, showy flowers that come in a wide range of colors. Their vibrant blooms and lush petals add a touch of elegance and charm to any garden.

2. FRAGRANCE:

Many peony varieties emit a delightful fragrance, adding a pleasant aroma to the garden. The sweet and enchanting scents of peonies can create a captivating sensory experience.

3. LONG BLOOMING PERIOD:

Peonies have a relatively long blooming period, typically lasting from late spring to early summer. This extended display of blooms ensures that the garden remains vibrant and colorful for an extended period.

4. LOW MAINTENANCE:

Peonies are relatively low maintenance plants, making them suitable for both experienced gardeners and beginners. Once established, they require minimal care and can thrive in various soil types and climates.

5. VERSATILITY:

Peonies can be grown in various garden settings, including borders, flower beds, and containers. They can also be used as cut flowers in floral arrangements, bringing their beauty indoors.

LANDSCAPE USES

Peonies have several landscape uses that make them valuable additions to garden designs:

1. FOCAL POINTS:

With their large and eye-catching flowers, peonies can serve as focal points in the garden. Placing them strategically in prominent locations can draw attention and create a visually stunning display.

2. BORDERS AND EDGES:

Peonies are often used to create borders and edges in flower beds and garden pathways. Their dense foliage *and beautiful flowers can define spaces and add structure to the landscape.*

3. MIXED PLANTINGS:

Peonies can be combined with other plants in mixed flower beds or perennial gardens. They pair well with perennials like irises, roses, and delphiniums, creating captivating color combinations and textural contrasts.

4. CUT FLOWER GARDENS:

Peonies are highly sought-after cut flowers due to their beauty and fragrance. Designating a specific area in the garden for growing peonies can provide a bountiful supply of blooms for floral arrangements.

Overall, the popularity of peonies as garden plants and their versatile landscape uses can be attributed to their stunning flowers, low maintenance requirements, and ability to enhance the visual appeal of any outdoor space.

PEONY

CULTURAL SIGNIFICANCE

Peonies hold significant cultural importance in various societies and traditions. Here are some examples of their cultural significance:

1. CHINESE CULTURE

In Chinese culture, the peony is regarded as the "King of Flowers" and holds deep cultural and symbolic meaning. It is considered a symbol of wealth, honor, and prosperity. Peonies are often depicted in Chinese art, textiles, and ceramics, representing beauty, grace, and good fortune. They are also associated with love and affection, making them popular flowers for weddings and romantic occasions.

2. JAPANESE CULTURE

In Japanese culture, the peony is known as "Botan" and is highly revered. It is considered a symbol of good fortune, bravery, and honor. Peonies are featured in traditional Japanese gardens and are celebrated during the "Peony Festival" held in various regions of Japan. The flowers are also associated with wealth and prosperity and are commonly used in traditional floral arrangements such as ikebana.

3. WESTERN CULTURE

In Western cultures, peonies are valued for their beauty and have been cultivated for centuries. In Victorian England, peonies symbolized bashfulness and represented the idea of a happy marriage. Today, they are cherished as ornamental plants and are often featured in gardens, bridal bouquets, and floral decorations. Peonies are also considered traditional flowers for the 12th wedding anniversary, symbolizing romance and prosperity.

4. MEDICAL AND HERBAL TRADITIONS

Peonies have a long history of medicinal and herbal use in various traditions. In traditional Chinese medicine, the roots of certain peony species are used for their therapeutic properties, believed to have a calming effect and to promote blood circulation. Peony root extracts are also used in herbal remedies for various ailments. In Western herbal medicine, peony has been used to alleviate pain and inflammation.

5. SYMBOLISM AND MYTHOLOGY

Peonies have been associated with mythological and symbolic meanings across cultures. In Greek mythology, Peon, the physician of the gods, was said to have used peony to heal the gods' wounds. In some cultures, peonies symbolize honor, abundance, and a happy life. They are also seen as a representation of feminine beauty and grace.

The cultural significance of peonies reflects their beauty, symbolism, and historical uses, making them an integral part of various societies and traditions.

PEONY

CULTIVATION AND PROPAGATION

Peonies can be cultivated and propagated through various methods. Here are some guidelines for their successful cultivation:

1. SITE SELECTION:

Choose a well-drained location with full sun or light shade for planting peonies. They prefer fertile soil that is rich in organic matter. Ensure that the planting site has good air circulation to prevent disease issues.

2. PLANTING:

Peonies are typically planted in the fall, allowing them to establish their root systems before the arrival of spring. Dig a hole that is wide and deep enough to accommodate the roots. Place the peony plant in the hole, making sure the eyes (buds) are positioned no more than 2 inches below the soil surface. Backfill the hole with soil and firm it gently around the plant.

3. WATERING:

Water newly planted peonies thoroughly after planting. Once established, they generally require about 1 inch of water per week, either from rainfall or supplemental watering. Avoid overwatering, as peonies are susceptible to root rot.

4. FERTILIZING:

In early spring, apply a balanced fertilizer specifically formulated for flowering plants around the peony plants. Follow the package instructions for the appropriate dosage. Avoid overfertilizing, as excessive nitrogen can result in lush foliage but fewer flowers.

5. SUPPORT:

As peonies produce large and heavy flowers, providing support for the plants is beneficial. Inserting stakes or using peony rings around the plants can help prevent them from flopping over and provide necessary support to the flower stems.

PROPAGATION:

Peonies can be propagated through several methods:

A. DIVISION:

Dividing mature peony plants is the most common method of propagation. This is usually done in early fall when the plants are dormant. Dig up the plant and carefully divide the root clump into sections, ensuring *each section has healthy buds and roots. Replant the divisions at the desired location.*

B. SEEDS:

Peonies can be grown from seeds, but this method is less commonly used as it takes several years for the plants to mature and bloom. Collect seeds from ripe peony seed pods in the fall, plant them in a well-draining seed-starting mix, and provide appropriate care until they develop into seedlings.

C. GRAFTING:

Grafting is another method used to propagate peonies. It involves joining a desired peony cultivar (scion) onto a rootstock of a different peony species. This technique is typically employed for propagating tree peonies and certain rare or delicate varieties.

By following these cultivation and propagation methods, you can successfully grow and propagate peonies to enjoy their beautiful flowers in your garden.

PEONY

IDEAL GROWING CONDITIONS AND SOIL REQUIREMENTS

Peonies thrive under specific growing conditions and have certain soil requirements for optimal growth. Here are the ideal conditions for growing peonies:

1. SUNLIGHT:

Peonies require full sun to produce abundant blooms. They should be planted in a location that receives at least 6 to 8 hours of direct sunlight each day. However, they can tolerate light shade, especially in hotter regions.

2. TEMPERATURE:

Peonies prefer cool to moderate climates. They are hardy in USDA hardiness zones 3 to 8. They require a period of winter dormancy with cold temperatures to initiate flower bud formation. However, some varieties can tolerate warmer climates if provided with sufficient shade and moisture.

3. SOIL TYPE:

Peonies prefer fertile, well-drained soil. They thrive in slightly acidic to neutral soil with a pH range of 6.5 to 7.5. The soil should have good drainage to prevent waterlogging, as excessive moisture can lead to root rot and other fungal diseases.

4. SOIL PREPARATION:

Before planting peonies, it is essential to prepare the soil properly. Amend heavy clay soil with organic matter such as compost or well-rotted manure to improve drainage and provide nutrients. Work the organic matter into the soil to a depth of 12 to 18 inches before planting.

5. MOISTURE:

While peonies prefer well-drained soil, they also require consistent moisture. Adequate watering is crucial, especially during the growing season and during periods of drought. Water deeply and thoroughly, ensuring the root zone receives sufficient moisture without becoming waterlogged.

6. AIR CIRCULATION:

Peonies benefit from good air circulation around the plants, as it helps prevent the development of fungal diseases. Avoid planting them in overcrowded areas or locations with poor air movement.

7. MULCHING:

Applying a layer of organic mulch around the base of peony plants can help conserve moisture, suppress weeds, and moderate soil temperatures. Use organic materials such as shredded bark, straw, or compost, and apply a layer about 2 to 3 inches deep, keeping it away from the crown of the plant.

By providing peonies with the ideal growing conditions and ensuring the soil meets their requirements, you can promote healthy growth and abundant blooms in your peony plants.

PEONY

IMPACT OF CLIMATE CHANGE

Climate change poses both direct and indirect impacts on peonies and their natural habitats. Here are some ways in which climate change can affect peonies:

1. SHIFTING GROWING ZONES:

As temperatures and climate patterns change, the suitable growing zones for peonies may shift. Warmer temperatures can push the boundaries of their traditional range, while changes in precipitation patterns can affect their water requirements.

2. ALTERED FLOWERING TIME:

Changes in temperature and seasonal patterns can disrupt the natural flowering time of peonies. Warmer winters and earlier springs can cause peonies to bloom prematurely or experience irregular flowering patterns.

3. INCREASED DISEASE AND PEST PRESSURE:

Climate change can create favorable conditions for the spread of pests and diseases that affect peonies. Rising temperatures and humidity levels can contribute to the proliferation of fungal diseases, such as botrytis blight, powdery mildew, and root rot.

4. HABITAT LOSS AND FRAGMENTATION:

Climate change can lead to habitat loss and fragmentation, affecting wild peony populations. Loss of suitable habitat, changes in precipitation patterns, and increased competition from invasive species can threaten the survival of certain peony species in their native habitats.

CONSERVATION EFFORTS

Efforts are underway to conserve and protect peony species in the face of climate change and other threats. Here are some conservation initiatives:

1. HABITAT PRESERVATION:

Conservation organizations and botanical gardens are working to protect and restore the natural habitats of peonies. This includes conserving areas with diverse peony species and implementing measures to mitigate habitat loss and fragmentation.

2. EX SITU CONSERVATION:

Botanical gardens and seed banks play a crucial role in ex situ conservation of peonies. They maintain *collections of peony species and varieties, preserving genetic diversity and ensuring their availability for future research and reintroduction efforts.*

3. RESEARCH AND MONITORING:

Scientists and researchers are studying the impact of climate change on peonies and their ecosystems. This research helps identify vulnerable populations, assess the genetic diversity of peony species, and develop conservation strategies to mitigate the effects of climate change.

4. CULTIVATION AND PROPAGATION:

Encouraging the cultivation and propagation of peonies in gardens and nurseries can help conserve and maintain a diverse range of peony varieties. This ensures the preservation of unique genetic traits and provides opportunities for reintroduction into the wild if necessary.

The combined efforts of conservation organizations, researchers, and gardening enthusiasts are vital for the conservation and protection of peonies in the face of climate change and other environmental challenges.

PEONY

SEASONAL CARE AND MAINTENANCE

Proper care and maintenance throughout the seasons are essential for the health and vigor of peony plants. Here are the seasonal care guidelines:

SPRING

Cutting Back Winter Debris: In early spring, remove any dead foliage and other winter debris around the peony plants. This helps prevent the spread of diseases and promotes new growth.

Supporting Stems: As the peony stems begin to emerge, provide support using stakes or peony rings. This will help prevent the heavy flower stems from bending or breaking as they grow.

Fertilizing: Apply a balanced fertilizer formulated for flowering plants around the base of the peony plants. Follow the package instructions for the recommended dosage.

SUMMER

Watering: Ensure that peonies receive sufficient water during dry periods. Water deeply, providing about 1 inch of water per week, either through rainfall or supplemental watering. Avoid overwatering to prevent root rot.

Weeding: Regularly remove weeds around the peony plants, as they can compete for nutrients and water. Use mulch to suppress weed growth and conserve soil moisture.

Deadheading: After the peony flowers fade, deadhead them by removing the spent blooms. This improves the plant's appearance and redirects energy toward root and foliage growth.

FALL

Dividing: Fall is the ideal time to divide mature peony plants. Carefully dig up the plant and divide the root clump into sections, ensuring each section has healthy buds and roots. Replant the divisions at the desired location.

Cutting Back Foliage: Once the foliage turns yellow or brown, cut it back to about 2 inches above the ground. This helps prevent the spread of diseases and prepares the plant for dormancy.

Applying Mulch: Apply a layer of organic mulch around the base of the peony plants in late fall. This helps insulate the soil, protect the roots from temperature fluctuations, and prevent weed growth.

WINTER

Protecting from Frost: In areas with severe winters, provide protection by mulching heavily around the base of the peony plants. This helps insulate the roots and prevent frost damage.

Monitoring: Monitor the plants during the winter months for any signs of pest or disease issues. Take necessary measures to address them promptly.

By following these seasonal care and maintenance practices, you can ensure the health and longevity of your peony plants, promoting beautiful blooms year after year.

PEONY

COMMON PESTS AND DISEASES

While peonies are generally resilient plants, they can be susceptible to certain pests and diseases. Here are some common issues to watch out for:

PESTS:

1. PEONY APHIDS

Aphids are small, soft-bodied insects that feed on the sap of peony plants. They can distort new growth and leave behind sticky honeydew. Natural predators like ladybugs can help control aphid populations, or you can use insecticidal soap or neem oil to treat infestations.

2. SPIDER MITES

Spider mites are tiny pests that suck the sap from peony leaves, causing yellowing, stippling, and webbing. Regularly spraying the foliage with water can help deter spider mites. If infestation occurs, use insecticidal soap or miticides to control them.

3. PEONY ERIOPHYID MITES

Eriophyid mites are microscopic pests that cause distorted and stunted growth in peony plants. Prune and destroy affected plant parts and consider applying horticultural oil to control these mites.

DISEASES:

1. BOTRYTIS BLIGHT (GRAY MOLD)

Botrytis blight is a fungal disease that affects peonies, especially in cool and humid conditions. It causes brown spots on leaves and buds, and infected flowers may turn mushy. To manage botrytis blight, remove and destroy affected plant parts, improve air circulation, and avoid overhead watering.

2. POWDERY MILDEW

Powdery mildew is a fungal disease that appears as a powdery white coating on leaves and stems. It can cause leaf distortion and stunted growth. To prevent powdery mildew, ensure good air circulation, avoid overhead watering, and apply fungicides if necessary.

3. PHYTOPHTHORA BLIGHT

Phytophthora blight is a soil-borne disease that can affect the roots and lower stems of peony plants. It causes wilting, yellowing, and crown rot. To prevent phytophthora blight, ensure well-drained soil, avoid overwatering, and practice proper sanitation measures.

4. VERTICILLIUM WILT

Verticillium wilt is a fungal disease that affects a wide range of plants, including peonies. It causes wilting, yellowing, and stunted growth. There is no cure for verticillium wilt, so prevention is crucial. Plant resistant cultivars and avoid planting peonies in soil where infected plants were present.

Regular monitoring, good cultural practices, and prompt action can help prevent and manage pest and disease issues in peonies. It's also beneficial to choose disease-resistant cultivars and ensure proper plant spacing and sanitation.

PEONY

POTENTIAL BENEFITS FOR PETS AND ANIMALS

Peonies offer various potential benefits for pets and animals in different ways. Here are some potential advantages:

1. NON-TOXICITY:

Peonies are generally considered non-toxic to pets, including cats and dogs. While it's always important to supervise pets around plants and ensure they don't ingest large quantities, the peony plant itself is not known to be highly toxic. However, it's still advisable to consult with a veterinarian if you suspect your pet has ingested any part of the peony plant.

2. ATTRACTING POLLINATORS:

Peony flowers are known to attract pollinators such as bees and butterflies. By planting peonies in your garden, you can provide a valuable food source for these beneficial insects, contributing to pollination and supporting local ecosystems.

3. SHELTER AND NESTING SITES:

The dense foliage of peony plants can provide shelter and nesting sites for small animals, such as birds and beneficial insects. The thick stems and leaves offer protection and a safe haven for wildlife to seek refuge or build nests.

4. ORNAMENTAL VALUE:

Peonies are beautiful flowering plants that can enhance the aesthetic appeal of your garden or outdoor space. The vibrant and showy blooms can attract visual interest, creating a pleasant environment for both humans and animals to enjoy.

5. ENVIRONMENTAL IMPACT:

By cultivating peonies and other plants in your garden, you contribute to a more biodiverse and environmentally-friendly landscape. Plants play a crucial role in maintaining ecological balance, providing habitat, improving air quality, and reducing soil erosion.

While the direct benefits of peonies for pets may be limited, their role in supporting pollinators, providing shelter, and enhancing the overall environment can have a positive impact on pets and animals indirectly.

PEONY

DANGER TO KIDS AND HOME PETS

Peonies are generally considered to have low toxicity levels, making them less dangerous to kids and home pets. Here are some important considerations:

NON-TOXIC PLANT:

Peonies are classified as non-toxic plants for humans and animals, including kids and home pets such as cats and dogs. While ingestion of any plant material should be monitored and excessive consumption avoided, the peony plant itself is not known to be highly toxic.

POTENTIAL MILD IRRITATION:

In some rare cases, mild irritation or allergic reactions may occur if the plant sap or pollen comes into contact with the skin or eyes. It's recommended to wash hands thoroughly after handling peonies or any plants to prevent potential irritation.

SUPERVISION AND CAUTION:

Although peonies are considered non-toxic, it's always important to exercise caution and supervise young children and pets around plants. Kids and pets may have different sensitivities or allergies, so it's advisable to consult with a healthcare professional or veterinarian if any concerns arise.

INGESTION AND CHOKING HAZARD:

While peonies are generally safe if ingested in small quantities, it's important to prevent young children and pets from consuming excessive amounts of any plant material. Ingesting large quantities of plant parts may cause gastrointestinal discomfort or other mild symptoms. If ingestion occurs, it's recommended to contact a healthcare professional or veterinarian for guidance.

PRECAUTIONS:

To minimize any potential risks, it's advisable to teach children not to eat or chew on plants and to keep an eye on pets to prevent them from excessively nibbling on peony plants or other vegetation. It's also recommended to consult with a healthcare professional or veterinarian if you suspect ingestion of large quantities or observe any concerning symptoms.

While peonies are generally safe, it's always important to exercise caution and take appropriate measures to ensure the safety of children and home pets around plants.

PEONY

STAGES OF GROWTH AND DEVELOPMENT: FROM SEED TO MATURE PLANT

Peonies undergo several distinct stages of growth and development throughout their life cycle. Here are the key stages:

1. SEED GERMINATION

Peonies can be grown from seeds, although this method is less common as it takes longer for the plants to mature. The seed germination process begins when a peony seed is planted in a suitable growing medium. Adequate moisture, temperature, and light conditions are essential for successful germination.

2. SEEDLING STAGE

After germination, the peony seed will develop into a seedling. During this stage, the plant will produce its first set of leaves, establishing its initial root system. Seedlings require careful attention to watering and light conditions to ensure healthy growth.

3. VEGETATIVE GROWTH

As the seedling grows, it enters the vegetative growth stage. The plant develops more leaves and begins to form a stronger root system. It focuses on foliage growth rather than flowering. This stage can last for several years, with the plant gradually increasing in size and vigor.

4. FLOWERING STAGE

Once the peony plant has reached maturity, it enters the flowering stage. This is the most anticipated and visually rewarding phase. Flower buds develop and open to reveal the characteristic large, colorful, and fragrant peony blooms. The flowering stage varies depending on the peony species or variety, typically occurring in late spring or early summer.

5. FRUITING AND SEED PRODUCTION

After the flowers have bloomed and faded, some peony varieties may produce seed pods. These pods contain seeds, allowing the plant to reproduce. Not all peonies produce viable seeds, and seed production is more common in herbaceous peonies compared to tree peonies.

6. DORMANCY

In autumn, peonies enter a period of dormancy. The above-ground foliage dies back, and the plant *becomes dormant for the winter months. This stage is essential for the plant's rest and rejuvenation, preparing it for the next growing season.*

Understanding the different stages of growth and development in peonies helps gardeners appreciate the plant's life cycle and implement appropriate care and maintenance practices throughout each stage.

PEONY

ROLE IN LANDSCAPING AND GARDEN DESIGN

Peonies play a significant role in landscaping and garden design, offering various benefits and enhancing the overall aesthetic appeal. Here are some key aspects of their role:

FOCAL POINT AND SHOWY BLOOMS

Peonies are often used as focal points in garden beds or as standalone plants due to their large, showy blooms. Their vibrant colors, intricate petal structures, and delightful fragrance make them eye-catching and visually stunning additions to any landscape.

SEASONAL INTEREST

Peonies provide a burst of color and beauty in the garden during their blooming season, typically in late spring or early summer. Their lush foliage adds visual interest even when not in bloom. By selecting different peony varieties with varying bloom times, it's possible to extend the flowering season and maintain garden interest throughout the spring and summer.

VERSATILE DESIGN OPTIONS

Peonies can be incorporated into various garden design styles, including formal gardens, cottage gardens, and naturalistic landscapes. They blend well with other perennials, annuals, and shrubs, allowing for diverse planting combinations and design possibilities.

BORDER PLANTINGS

Peonies make excellent choices for border plantings, creating a stunning display along garden edges or pathways. Their upright growth habit and attractive foliage provide structure and define garden borders, adding depth and visual appeal to the overall design.

CUT FLOWER GARDENS

Peonies are highly valued for their use as cut flowers in floral arrangements. Including peony plants in a dedicated cut flower garden allows for the abundant harvest of these beautiful blooms. Their long stems and luxurious flowers make them sought-after additions to bouquets and floral designs.

LOW MAINTENANCE PERENNIALS

Peonies are relatively low maintenance perennials once established. Their longevity and resilience make them ideal for long-term garden design plans. With proper care and suitable growing conditions, peonies *can thrive for many years, providing lasting beauty and enjoyment.*

Whether used as focal points, border plantings, or as part of a larger garden design, peonies offer versatility, elegance, and enduring beauty, enhancing the overall landscape and delighting garden enthusiasts.

PEONY

DIFFERENT USES IN GARDENING

Peonies have multiple uses in gardening, offering versatility and beauty in various contexts. Here are some common uses of peonies in garden settings:

1. BEDDING PLANTS

Peonies are often used as bedding plants, adding color, texture, and visual interest to garden beds and borders. Their large, showy blooms create a striking display and can serve as focal points within a larger planting scheme.

2. CUT FLOWERS

Peonies are highly valued for their use as cut flowers. Their beautiful blooms make exquisite floral arrangements and bouquets, bringing elegance and fragrance indoors. Whether used in professional floral arrangements or enjoyed in home flower arrangements, peonies are a popular choice for their long-lasting and captivating blooms.

3. CONTAINER PLANTS

Peonies can be grown in containers, allowing for flexibility in garden design and placement. Container-grown peonies can be placed on patios, balconies, or other outdoor spaces, adding a touch of elegance and charm to these areas. It's important to select appropriate container sizes to accommodate the root system and ensure proper drainage.

4. HERBACEOUS BORDERS

Peonies make excellent additions to herbaceous borders, where they can be interplanted with other perennial flowers and ornamental grasses. Their long-lasting blooms provide a burst of color and create a lush and vibrant border. Combining peonies with complementary plants can result in a visually stunning and harmonious garden design.

5. NATURALISTIC LANDSCAPES

Peonies can be incorporated into naturalistic or cottage-style landscapes, contributing to the overall aesthetic appeal and creating a romantic and whimsical atmosphere. Their soft colors and delicate blooms blend seamlessly with other flowering plants, grasses, and native species, providing a natural and effortless beauty.

With their versatility and ability to thrive in different garden settings, peonies offer an array of uses in *gardening, whether as bedding plants, cut flowers, container plants, or as part of various landscape designs.*

PEONY

PRESERVING AND DRYING PEONY PLANTS FOR DECORATIVE PURPOSES

Peony flowers can be preserved and dried to extend their beauty and use them for decorative purposes. Here are different methods you can use:

1. AIR DRYING

Air drying is a simple and popular method to preserve peony blooms. Follow these steps:

1. Choose peonies that are at their peak bloom but not fully opened.
2. Cut the stems at an angle and remove excess foliage.
3. Gather a few stems together and secure them with a rubber band or string.
4. Hang the bundled peonies upside down in a dark, dry, and well-ventilated area.
5. Allow the flowers to dry completely, which can take a few weeks or more.
6. Once dried, you can use the preserved peonies in dried flower arrangements or other decorative crafts.

2. SILICA GEL DRYING

Using silica gel is another effective method for drying peony flowers while maintaining their shape and color. Here's how to do it:

1. Select peonies with tight buds or semi-open blooms.
2. Prepare a container deep enough to accommodate the flowers and silica gel.
3. Pour a layer of silica gel into the container.
4. Trim the peony stems and place the flowers face up in the container.
5. Gently pour more silica gel around and over the flowers, making sure to cover them completely.
6. Seal the container with a lid and let it sit undisturbed for about one to two weeks.
7. Once the drying period is complete, carefully remove the peonies from the silica gel, brushing off any excess gel.
8. The preserved peonies can be used in arrangements or displayed as dried flowers.

3. PRESSING

Pressing is a method that allows you to preserve peony flowers flat, making them suitable for various crafts. Here's what you need to do:

1. Choose peonies with relatively flat blooms and remove the stems.
2. Place the flowers between layers of absorbent paper or parchment paper.
3. Put the paper with the flowers inside a heavy book or flower press.
4. Apply additional weight on top of the book or press, if needed.
5. Leave the peonies pressed for several weeks, replacing the paper periodically if it becomes damp.
6. Once the flowers are fully dried and pressed, they can be used for pressed flower art, cards, or other decorative crafts.

By using these preservation methods, you can enjoy the beauty of peonies long after their natural blooming season, adding a touch of elegance to your home decor or special occasions.

PEONY

HYBRIDIZATION AND BREEDING TECHNIQUES FOR CREATING NEW PLANT VARIETIES

Peonies can be selectively hybridized and bred to create new plant varieties with desired traits. Here are some techniques commonly used in peony breeding:

1. HAND POLLINATION

Hand pollination is a manual technique where breeders transfer pollen from the stamen of one peony flower to the stigma of another, controlled plant. This technique allows breeders to carefully select the parent plants based on their desired characteristics, such as flower color, form, size, and fragrance.

2. CONTROLLED CROSS-POLLINATION

In controlled cross-pollination, breeders protect the chosen parent plants from unwanted pollen sources, ensuring that only the desired pollen is used in the breeding process. This technique helps maintain genetic purity and control the traits passed on to the offspring.

3. SELECTION AND EVALUATION

After cross-pollination, breeders evaluate the resulting seedlings for desirable traits. This involves assessing characteristics such as flower color, form, size, fragrance, stem length, disease resistance, and overall plant vigor. The selection process may take several years, with only the most promising seedlings advancing to the next stages of breeding.

4. PROPAGATION AND CLONING

Once a desirable seedling is identified, breeders propagate and clone the plant to ensure its consistent characteristics in subsequent generations. This is often done through vegetative propagation methods such as division, where the root system is carefully divided into multiple sections, each giving rise to a genetically identical plant.

5. RECOMBINATION AND HYBRID VIGOR

Hybridization introduces genetic recombination, resulting in offspring that exhibit hybrid vigor or heterosis. Hybrid vigor refers to the increased growth, vigor, and overall performance of hybrid plants compared to their parent plants. Breeders capitalize on this phenomenon to develop peony varieties with improved traits and increased vigor.

6. MULTI-GENERATION BREEDING

Breeders often conduct multi-generation breeding programs, where selected hybrids are further crossed with other desirable parents. This process allows for the refinement and enhancement of specific traits while maintaining genetic diversity and introducing new combinations of genes.

Through these hybridization and breeding techniques, peony breeders strive to create new plant varieties that exhibit superior characteristics, including improved flower colors, forms, sizes, disease resistance, and overall garden performance.

PEONY

ROLE OF PEONY IN TRADITIONAL MEDICINAL PRACTICES AND HERBAL REMEDIES

Peony has a long history of use in traditional medicinal practices and herbal remedies. It is highly regarded for its therapeutic properties and is utilized in various forms. Here are some ways peony is used in traditional medicine:

1. TRADITIONAL CHINESE MEDICINE (TCM)

In Traditional Chinese Medicine, peony root (Paeonia lactiflora) is commonly used. It is known as "Bai Shao" and is believed to have several medicinal benefits. Some traditional uses include:

- Harmonizing the blood and relieving pain
- Calming the liver and nourishing the blood
- Regulating menstruation and relieving menstrual pain
- Reducing muscle cramps and spasms
- Supporting liver health and reducing inflammation

2. AYURVEDIC MEDICINE

In Ayurvedic medicine, peony is known as "Saraca" or "Saraca asoka." Different parts of the plant, including the root, bark, and flowers, are used for their medicinal properties. Some traditional uses in Ayurveda include:

- Treating gynecological disorders
- Supporting reproductive health
- Alleviating menstrual discomfort
- Strengthening the uterus
- Calming the mind and reducing anxiety

3. HERBAL REMEDIES

In Western herbal medicine, peony is valued for its anti-inflammatory and analgesic properties. It is used in herbal remedies for conditions such as:

- Relieving muscle cramps and spasms
- Alleviating menstrual pain
- Supporting hormonal balance
- Reducing inflammation associated with conditions like arthritis
- Promoting relaxation and reducing stress

4. OTHER TRADITIONAL USES

Peony has also been used in various other traditional medicinal practices around the world. In some cultures, it has been employed for its astringent, anti-inflammatory, and analgesic properties.

While peony has a rich history in traditional medicine, it's important to note that the information provided here is for informational purposes only. Consultation with a *qualified healthcare professional is essential before using peony or any other herb for medicinal purposes.*

PEONY

CHALLENGES AND COMMON MISTAKES IN GROWING PEONY PLANTS

Growing peony plants can come with its challenges, but with proper care and attention, these challenges can be overcome. Here are some common mistakes and ways to overcome them:

1. IMPROPER PLANTING DEPTH

Planting peonies too deep or too shallow can hinder their growth and flowering. To overcome this:

- Ensure that the peony's eyes (buds) are planted no more than 2 inches below the soil surface.
- In regions with hot climates, consider planting the peony slightly deeper, around 2 to 3 inches below the soil surface.

2. INSUFFICIENT SUNLIGHT

Peonies require at least 6 hours of direct sunlight per day to thrive and produce abundant blooms. To overcome insufficient sunlight:

- Choose a planting location that receives full sun or light shade.
- Prune surrounding trees or shrubs that may cast shade over the peony plants.

3. OVERWATERING OR POOR DRAINAGE

Peonies prefer well-draining soil and can suffer from root rot if overwatered or planted in poorly drained areas. To overcome this:

- Ensure the planting site has good drainage or amend the soil with organic matter to improve drainage.
- Water peonies deeply but infrequently, allowing the soil to dry out slightly between waterings.

4. LACK OF SUPPORT FOR BLOOMS

The heavy blooms of peony plants may require support to prevent them from drooping or falling over. To overcome this:

- Install peony supports or cages around the plants in early spring, before they start growing vigorously.
- Gently tie the stems to the support structure as the plants grow, using soft twine or plant ties.

5. FAILURE TO DIVIDE OVERCROWDED PLANTS

Over time, peony plants can become overcrowded, resulting in reduced blooming. To overcome this:

- Divide mature peony plants every 4 to 5 years, preferably in early fall.
- Carefully dig up the plant, separate the clumps, and replant them at the appropriate depth and spacing.

By being mindful of these common mistakes and taking the necessary steps to overcome them, you can ensure the successful growth and beautiful blooms of your peony plants.

PEONY

CHALLENGES IN CONSERVATION AND PRESERVATION OF PEONY PLANTS

Peony plants face several challenges when it comes to their conservation and preservation. These challenges can impact the long-term survival and availability of different peony species and varieties. Here are some key challenges:

1. HABITAT LOSS AND FRAGMENTATION

The destruction and fragmentation of natural habitats are significant threats to peony populations. Human activities such as agriculture, urbanization, and infrastructure development can result in the loss of suitable habitats for peonies. This loss of habitat restricts their growth and reproduction, leading to population decline.

2. EXPLOITATION AND OVERCOLLECTION

Peonies are often targeted for their ornamental value, medicinal properties, and cut flowers, which can lead to overcollection from the wild. Unregulated harvesting practices can deplete wild populations and disrupt natural ecosystems. It is crucial to promote sustainable harvesting practices and discourage the illegal collection of peonies from their natural habitats.

3. CLIMATE CHANGE

Climate change poses significant challenges to peony conservation. Alterations in temperature, precipitation patterns, and extreme weather events can impact the growth, flowering, and overall health of peony plants. Changes in climate conditions may also disrupt the mutualistic relationships between peonies and their pollinators, affecting their reproductive success.

4. INVASIVE SPECIES

Invasive plant species can outcompete and displace native peony populations, leading to their decline. Invasive plants can negatively affect the availability of resources, alter ecosystem dynamics, and disrupt the natural balance required for the survival of native peonies. Controlling and managing invasive species is essential to protect peony habitats.

5. LACK OF CONSERVATION EFFORTS AND AWARENESS

Insufficient conservation efforts and limited awareness about the importance of peony conservation pose challenges. Conservation initiatives, such as establishing protected areas, promoting sustainable cultivation, and raising public awareness about the value of peonies in ecosystems and cultural heritage, are crucial for their long-term preservation.

6. GENETIC EROSION

Genetic erosion is a significant concern for peony conservation. Limited genetic diversity within populations can make them more vulnerable to diseases, pests, and environmental changes. Efforts should be made to preserve and maintain diverse gene pools of peony species and varieties to ensure their resilience and adaptability to changing conditions.

Addressing these challenges requires collaborative efforts involving conservation organizations, researchers, policymakers, and the public. By implementing conservation strategies, promoting sustainable practices, and raising awareness about the importance of peony preservation, we can work towards securing the future of these beautiful and valuable plants.

PEONY

SYMBOLISM OF PEONY IN WEDDINGS AND CELEBRATIONS

Peony holds significant symbolism in weddings and celebrations, representing various meanings and emotions. It is often regarded as a symbol of love, romance, prosperity, and happiness. Here are some symbolic associations of peony in different cultures and traditions:

1. LOVE AND ROMANCE

In many cultures, peony is considered a flower of love and romance. It symbolizes deep affection, passion, and a happy marriage. Peonies are often incorporated into wedding bouquets, bridal arrangements, and decorations to convey love and express the joy of matrimony.

2. PROSPERITY AND WEALTH

Peonies are associated with prosperity, abundance, and good fortune. Their lush blooms and vibrant colors are seen as a symbol of wealth and success. In celebrations and festive occasions, peonies are used to bring luck, prosperity, and a flourishing future.

3. BEAUTY AND ELEGANCE

The beauty and elegance of peony flowers make them a symbol of grace, refinement, and femininity. They are admired for their large, showy blooms and delicate petals, representing beauty and charm. Peonies are often chosen for bridal bouquets and centerpieces to add a touch of elegance and sophistication to weddings and celebrations.

4. HONOR AND RESPECT

In some cultures, peonies symbolize honor, respect, and nobility. They are associated with qualities such as dignity, integrity, and high social status. Peonies may be used in ceremonial settings or presented as gifts to convey honor and show respect to esteemed individuals.

5. NEW BEGINNINGS AND GOOD WISHES

Peonies are also seen as a symbol of new beginnings and fresh starts. They represent hope, optimism, and positive energy. In weddings and celebrations, peonies are used to celebrate new chapters in life, such as the start of a marriage, the birth of a child, or the beginning of a prosperous journey.

The symbolism of peony in weddings and celebrations varies across cultures and traditions, but its association with love, prosperity, beauty, and new beginnings remains a common thread. The presence of peonies in special occasions adds a touch of symbolism and meaningfulness, enhancing the overall atmosphere and significance of the event.

PEONY

ROLE OF PEONY PLANTS IN BIODIVERSITY CONSERVATION AND CONTRIBUTION TO LOCAL ECOSYSTEMS

Peony plants play a significant role in biodiversity conservation and contribute to the health and balance of local ecosystems. Here are some key points highlighting their importance:

1. HABITAT AND NECTAR SOURCE

Peonies serve as important habitat and nectar sources for various pollinators, including bees, butterflies, and other beneficial insects. The abundant and fragrant blooms of peony plants attract pollinators, supporting their populations and contributing to the pollination of other plants in the ecosystem.

2. FOOD SOURCE FOR WILDLIFE

The seeds of peony plants serve as a food source for certain bird species, contributing to their diet and overall biodiversity. Birds such as finches and sparrows are known to feed on peony seeds, helping to disperse them and promote the growth of new peony plants in different areas.

3. SOIL STABILIZATION

The extensive root systems of peony plants aid in soil stabilization. Their deep and fibrous roots help prevent soil erosion and improve soil structure, particularly in areas with loose or vulnerable soils. This contributes to the overall stability of the ecosystem and protects against land degradation.

4. DIVERSITY AND RESILIENCE

Peonies add to the overall diversity and resilience of local ecosystems. Their presence enhances the floral diversity and provides a unique habitat for specialized organisms. By supporting a variety of pollinators and wildlife, peonies contribute to the ecological balance and resilience of the ecosystem.

5. CULTURAL AND TRADITIONAL SIGNIFICANCE

Peonies hold cultural and traditional significance in many societies. Their cultivation and preservation help maintain cultural heritage and traditional practices. Conserving peonies as part of the local flora contributes to the cultural and aesthetic value of the landscape, enriching the connection between people and nature.

By recognizing the role of peony plants in biodiversity conservation and their contributions to local ecosystems, efforts can be made to protect and preserve these valuable plants. Promoting sustainable cultivation, conserving natural habitats, and raising awareness about the ecological importance of peonies can help ensure their continued presence and benefits to local biodiversity.

PEONY

TRADITIONAL USES OF PEONY IN BEAUTY AND COSMETICS

Peony has been utilized in beauty and cosmetics for its beneficial properties and soothing effects on the skin. Throughout history, various parts of the peony plant have been incorporated into traditional beauty practices. Here are some traditional uses of peony in beauty and cosmetics:

1. SKIN BRIGHTENING AND COMPLEXION ENHANCEMENT

Peony extracts and infusions have been used to brighten the skin and enhance the complexion. The natural compounds present in peony, such as flavonoids and antioxidants, are believed to help improve skin tone, reduce uneven pigmentation, and promote a more radiant appearance.

2. ANTI-INFLAMMATORY AND SOOTHING PROPERTIES

Peony has long been recognized for its anti-inflammatory and soothing properties. Preparations made from peony roots or petals have been used topically to calm irritated skin, reduce redness, and alleviate skin conditions such as acne, eczema, and rosacea.

3. MOISTURIZING AND HYDRATING EFFECTS

Peony extracts and oils are known for their moisturizing and hydrating effects on the skin. They are often included in skincare products such as creams, lotions, and serums to provide deep hydration, improve skin elasticity, and promote a smoother and more supple complexion.

4. ASTRINGENT AND TONING PROPERTIES

Peony has astringent properties, which can help tighten and tone the skin. Traditional preparations made from peony have been used as natural toners to minimize the appearance of pores, balance oil production, and promote a more refined and even skin texture.

5. FRAGRANCE AND PERFUME INGREDIENT

Peony's enchanting fragrance has made it a popular ingredient in perfumes and fragrances. The delicate and floral scent of peony adds a refreshing and feminine touch to various cosmetic products, including perfumes, soaps, and bath products.

While peony has a rich history in traditional beauty and cosmetic practices, it's important to note that the effectiveness of these traditional uses may vary, and individual experiences may differ. It is advisable to consult with skincare professionals or dermatologists before incorporating peony-based products into your beauty routine.

PEONY

CULINARY USES OF PEONY IN FOOD AND BEVERAGES

While peony is primarily known for its ornamental and medicinal properties, certain parts of the plant have also been used in culinary practices for their unique flavors and aromas. Here are some culinary uses of peony:

1. EDIBLE FLOWERS

The vibrant and fragrant flowers of peony can be used as edible decorations in various dishes. The petals can be added to salads, desserts, or beverages to provide a visually appealing and aromatic touch. It is important to note that only certain peony varieties are considered safe for consumption, so proper identification is necessary before using peony flowers in food.

2. HERBAL TEAS

Peony petals and roots are often used to make herbal teas. The petals can be dried and steeped to create a fragrant and soothing tea with a subtle floral flavor. Peony root tea, also known as "bai shao cha" in traditional Chinese medicine, is known for its calming properties and is believed to support overall well-being.

3. FLAVORING AND INFUSIONS

Peony petals can be used to infuse flavor into culinary creations. The petals can be added to syrups, jellies, or infused oils to impart a delicate floral essence. Peony-infused ingredients can be incorporated into cakes, pastries, and other desserts to add a unique and aromatic touch.

4. TRADITIONAL MEDICINE INGREDIENTS

Peony roots are used as an ingredient in traditional medicine, particularly in East Asian cuisines. In Chinese cuisine, peony roots are sometimes added to soups or stews for their believed health benefits. It is important to note that the usage of peony roots in culinary practices for medicinal purposes should be done under the guidance of knowledgeable practitioners.

When using peony in culinary applications, it is essential to ensure the safety and suitability of the specific peony variety and parts being used. As with any culinary ingredient, it is recommended to research and follow proper guidelines and recipes to fully appreciate the unique flavors and potential benefits of peony in food and beverages.

PEONY

USE OF PEONY PLANTS IN CRAFTS

Peony plants have been valued not only for their beauty but also for their versatile use in various crafts. The different parts of the peony plant can be incorporated into creative projects, adding a touch of elegance and natural charm. Here are some ways peony plants are used in crafts:

1. FLOWER ARRANGEMENTS AND FLORAL CRAFTS

Peony flowers are highly sought after for flower arrangements and floral crafts. Their large, showy blooms and captivating colors make them a popular choice for bouquets, centerpieces, wreaths, and other decorative displays. Peony petals can also be preserved and used in pressed flower crafts or potpourri.

2. PAPERMAKING AND STATIONERY

The delicate beauty of peony flowers inspires the creation of handmade papers and stationery. Peony petals or images of peonies can be used in papermaking to add a decorative element. Handcrafted peony-themed stationery, including greeting cards, invitations, and bookmarks, can be created to convey a sense of elegance and charm.

3. DYEING AND FABRIC CRAFTS

Peony petals can be used to create natural dyes for fabric and fiber crafts. By boiling the petals and extracting their pigments, various shades of pink, purple, and red can be achieved. These natural dyes can be used to color textiles, yarns, or even create unique tie-dye patterns, adding a touch of botanical beauty to fabric-based crafts.

4. POTTERY AND CERAMIC DECORATION

Peony flowers and motifs are often depicted in pottery and ceramic art. The elegant and graceful form of peonies lends itself well to decorative ceramics, such as vases, plates, and tiles. Peony-inspired designs can be hand-painted or incorporated into ceramic molds, showcasing the timeless beauty of these flowers in artistic creations.

5. JEWELRY AND ACCESSORIES

Peony flowers can inspire the design of jewelry and accessories. Peony petals or resin casts of peony blooms can be used to create unique pendants, earrings, brooches, and hair accessories. The intricate details and symbolic meanings associated with *peonies can be translated into wearable art, making a statement piece for nature enthusiasts.*

The use of peony plants in crafts allows for a creative exploration of their beauty and symbolism. Whether it's through floral arrangements, papermaking, natural dyeing, ceramic decoration, or jewelry making, peonies provide endless possibilities for incorporating their charm into various craft projects.

PEONY

MYTHS AND LEGENDS SURROUNDING PEONY IN DIFFERENT CULTURES

Peony plants have captured the imagination and inspired numerous myths and legends in different cultures throughout history. These stories often depict peonies as symbols of beauty, love, prosperity, and various other virtues. Here are some examples of the myths and legends surrounding peonies:

1. ANCIENT GREEK MYTHOLOGY: THE ORIGIN OF PEONIES

In ancient Greek mythology, it is believed that the peony was named after Paeon, a physician to the gods. According to the myth, Paeon used a peony root to heal a wounded god, and from the blood of the wounded god, the first peony flower bloomed. The peony became associated with healing and medicinal properties.

2. CHINESE MYTHOLOGY: THE FLOWER OF WEALTH AND PROSPERITY

In Chinese culture, peonies are regarded as the "King of Flowers" and have deep cultural significance. According to a Chinese legend, peonies are associated with wealth and prosperity. It is believed that planting peony flowers in your garden will bring good fortune and abundance.

3. JAPANESE MYTHOLOGY: THE GODDESS OF PEONIES

In Japanese folklore, there is a myth surrounding the goddess of peonies known as Botan Dōrō. According to the legend, a beautiful woman named Botan was turned into a peony flower as a punishment for her pride. It is said that peonies blossomed wherever she walked, and she became a symbol of beauty and elegance.

4. PERSIAN MYTHOLOGY: THE TALE OF THE NIGHTINGALE AND THE PEONY

In Persian mythology, there is a tale of a nightingale that fell in love with a peony flower. The nightingale was so enchanted by the beauty and fragrance of the peony that it could not bear to leave its side. This story symbolizes the eternal love and devotion between the nightingale and the peony.

5. EUROPEAN FOLKLORE: LEGENDS OF FAIRIES AND MAGICAL POWERS

In European folklore, peonies are often associated with fairies and magical powers. It was believed that if you planted peonies in your garden, the fairies would be drawn to them and bless your home with their presence. Peonies were also thought to possess protective qualities against evil spirits and were used to ward off negative energies.

These myths and legends surrounding peonies showcase the cultural significance and enduring fascination with these captivating flowers. They highlight the symbolic meanings attributed to peonies and their representation of beauty, love, prosperity, and enchantment in various cultures.

PEONY

METHODS OF USING PEONY IN AROMATHERAPY

Peony plants not only captivate with their beauty but also offer a delicate and soothing fragrance that can be utilized in aromatherapy. The aromatic compounds found in peonies can help create a calming and relaxing atmosphere. Here are some methods of using peony in aromatherapy:

1. ESSENTIAL OIL

Peony essential oil is extracted from the petals of the peony flower through a distillation process. The oil carries the pleasant and gentle floral scent of peonies. It can be used in aromatherapy by adding a few drops to a diffuser or oil burner to create a tranquil ambiance. Inhaling the aroma of peony essential oil may help promote relaxation and reduce stress.

2. POTPOURRI AND SACHETS

Dried peony petals can be used in potpourri or sachets to infuse spaces with their subtle fragrance. Simply combine dried peony petals with other aromatic ingredients such as dried herbs, spices, or essential oils, and place them in decorative bowls or small fabric pouches. These can be placed in closets, drawers, or around the house to provide a pleasant and calming scent.

3. BATH AND BODY PRODUCTS

Peony fragrance can be incorporated into bath and body products to create a luxurious and soothing experience. Peony-scented soaps, bath salts, shower gels, lotions, and candles can be used to indulge in the calming aroma while taking a bath or pampering oneself. The gentle floral notes of peony can contribute to a serene and rejuvenating ambiance.

4. FLORAL WATERS AND MISTS

Peony floral waters, also known as hydrosols, are made by steam distilling peony flowers. These floral waters contain the aromatic properties of the plant and can be used as refreshing facial mists or linen sprays. They can help revitalize the skin, provide a delicate scent, and create a soothing atmosphere in your surroundings.

5. AROMATHERAPY BLENDS

Peony fragrance can be blended with other essential oils or natural scents to create unique aromatherapy blends. Combining peony with calming essential oils such as lavender, chamomile, or ylang-ylang can *enhance relaxation and promote a sense of tranquility. These blends can be used in diffusers, massage oils, or personal inhalers.*

When using peony in aromatherapy, it's important to ensure that you are using high-quality and properly diluted products. If you have any sensitivities or allergies, it's advisable to perform a patch test before using peony-based aromatherapy products extensively.

The delicate and soothing fragrance of peonies offers a natural way to enhance relaxation and create a serene environment in aromatherapy practices.

PEONY

CHEMICAL COMPOSITION AND MEDICINAL PROPERTIES OF PEONY

Peony plants (Paeonia spp.) contain various chemical compounds that contribute to their medicinal properties. These compounds are found in different parts of the plant, including the roots, leaves, and flowers. Here are some key components of the chemical composition of peony and their associated medicinal properties:

1. PAEONIFLORIN

Paeoniflorin is one of the major active compounds found in peony roots. It possesses anti-inflammatory, antioxidant, and neuroprotective properties. Paeoniflorin has been studied for its potential benefits in reducing inflammation, relieving pain, and improving cognitive function.

2. PAEONOL

Paeonol is a phenolic compound present in peony bark and flowers. It exhibits antioxidant and anti-inflammatory effects. Paeonol has been investigated for its potential use in skincare products due to its ability to protect against oxidative stress and promote skin health.

3. TRITERPENOIDS

Triterpenoids are bioactive compounds found in peony roots and flowers. They have shown anti-inflammatory, antitumor, and immunomodulatory properties. Triterpenoids are believed to contribute to the traditional medicinal uses of peony, including its potential benefits for pain relief and immune system support.

4. FLAVONOIDS

Peony plants contain various flavonoids, such as quercetin and kaempferol, which possess antioxidant and anti-inflammatory properties. These flavonoids contribute to the overall therapeutic effects of peony and may have a positive impact on human health.

5. ESSENTIAL OILS

The essential oil derived from peony flowers contains aromatic compounds that have a soothing and calming effect. These oils may have a mild sedative effect and can be used in aromatherapy to promote relaxation and reduce stress and anxiety.

The medicinal properties of peony are diverse, and they have been traditionally used in herbal medicine for various purposes. However, it's important to note that while peony has a long history of traditional use, further scientific research is needed to fully understand and validate its medicinal potential.

PEONY

THERAPEUTIC USES OF PEONY FOR HUMANS

Peony plants (Paeonia spp.) have a long history of traditional use in herbal medicine for various therapeutic purposes. While further scientific research is needed to fully validate these uses, peony is believed to offer several potential benefits for human health. Here are some therapeutic uses associated with peony:

1. ANTI-INFLAMMATORY PROPERTIES

Peony has been traditionally used for its anti-inflammatory properties. Compounds like paeoniflorin and triterpenoids found in peony exhibit anti-inflammatory effects. These properties make peony a potential natural remedy for inflammatory conditions such as arthritis, rheumatism, and inflammatory skin disorders.

2. PAIN RELIEF

Due to its anti-inflammatory properties, peony may also offer pain-relieving effects. Traditional medicine has used peony for alleviating pain associated with conditions such as menstrual cramps, muscle aches, and joint pain. However, further research is necessary to understand the specific mechanisms and efficacy of peony in pain management.

3. SKIN HEALTH

Peony is known for its potential benefits in promoting skin health. Paeonol, an active compound found in peony, exhibits antioxidant and anti-inflammatory properties, which may contribute to its skin-soothing effects. Peony extracts or products containing peony are used in skincare formulations for their potential to reduce redness, irritation, and oxidative damage.

4. MOOD AND STRESS MANAGEMENT

The gentle and calming fragrance of peony flowers is often associated with relaxation and stress relief. Aromatherapy using peony essential oil or dried peony petals may help promote a sense of calmness, alleviate anxiety, and enhance mood. Inhaling the soothing aroma of peony may contribute to a relaxed state of mind.

5. TRADITIONAL CHINESE MEDICINE (TCM) USES

In Traditional Chinese Medicine, peony is highly regarded for its therapeutic properties. It is used to tonify the blood, regulate menstrual cycles, and soothe liver and abdominal discomfort. Peony is often *included in herbal formulas for conditions such as menstrual disorders, menopausal symptoms, and liver imbalances.*

While peony shows promise for various therapeutic uses, it's important to consult with a healthcare professional or qualified herbalist before using peony for medicinal purposes. They can provide personalized guidance and ensure its safe and appropriate use.

PEONY

ROLE OF PEONY IN MODERN CULTURE

Peony plants (Paeonia spp.) have gained significant popularity and play various roles in modern culture. They are cherished for their beauty, symbolism, and versatility. Here are some aspects highlighting the role of peony in modern culture:

1. ORNAMENTAL AND FLORAL DESIGN

Peonies are highly valued as ornamental plants in gardens, parks, and floral arrangements. Their large, showy blooms and diverse color range make them sought-after flowers for weddings, celebrations, and other special occasions. Peonies are often featured in floral design and contribute to the aesthetics and elegance of modern floral arrangements.

2. SYMBOLISM AND TRADITIONS

Peonies hold symbolic meanings in different cultures and traditions. They are associated with beauty, prosperity, honor, and romance. In Chinese culture, peonies are known as the "king of flowers" and symbolize wealth, happiness, and a prosperous future. Peony festivals and events celebrate their beauty and cultural significance, fostering a sense of community and tradition.

3. ART AND LITERATURE

Peonies have inspired artists, writers, and poets throughout history. Their captivating blooms and rich symbolism often find expression in paintings, sculptures, poetry, and literature. Peonies are celebrated for their beauty and used as metaphors for love, femininity, and the fleeting nature of life in various artistic and literary works.

4. COMMERCIAL AND ECONOMIC IMPORTANCE

The popularity of peonies as ornamental plants has contributed to a thriving commercial industry. Peony cultivation, trade, and sales have become economically significant in many regions. Peonies are grown for cut flower production, landscaping, and the horticultural market, generating revenue and employment opportunities.

5. CULTURAL FESTIVALS AND EVENTS

Peony festivals and garden tours have gained prominence as cultural events. These events attract visitors and enthusiasts who come to admire the diverse displays of peony cultivars, participate in flower shows, and learn about the history and cultural *significance of peonies. Such festivals promote tourism, cultural exchange, and community engagement.*

Peonies have firmly established themselves in modern culture, captivating people with their beauty, symbolism, and contributions to various artistic, economic, and cultural spheres.

PEONY

WAYS TO ENJOY AND APPRECIATE PEONY

Peony plants (Paeonia spp.) offer several ways to enjoy and appreciate their beauty and unique characteristics. Here are different ways to experience and appreciate peonies:

1. GARDEN CULTIVATION

Grow peonies in your garden or backyard to witness their stunning blooms up close. Select from a wide range of peony varieties, including herbaceous, tree, and intersectional peonies, and create a dedicated peony garden bed or incorporate them into existing flower beds. Observe their growth stages, from emerging shoots to lush foliage and magnificent flowers.

2. CUT FLOWERS

Cut peony flowers and bring them indoors to enjoy their beauty and fragrance. Create vibrant floral arrangements for your home or use peonies as centerpieces for special occasions and celebrations. Peonies make excellent cut flowers due to their large blooms and long vase life, allowing you to appreciate their beauty indoors.

3. FLORAL DESIGN

Engage in floral design and incorporate peonies into your floral creations. Explore various arrangements, bouquets, and installations where peonies can take center stage or be combined with other complementary flowers and foliage. Let your creativity flourish as you showcase the elegance and charm of peonies in your floral designs.

4. PHOTOGRAPHY

Capture the captivating beauty of peonies through photography. Whether you're an amateur or professional photographer, peonies provide an excellent subject with their intricate petals, vibrant colors, and delicate details. Experiment with different angles, lighting conditions, and compositions to showcase the unique characteristics of peonies through your lens.

5. NATURE WALKS AND GARDEN TOURS

Embark on nature walks or visit public gardens and parks renowned for their peony collections. Enjoy the serene beauty of peonies in their natural habitat and learn about different varieties and cultivars. Many botanical gardens organize peony festivals and guided tours, providing opportunities to appreciate the diversity and magnificence of these plants.

6. PAINTING AND ARTISTIC EXPRESSION

Express your creativity through art by painting or drawing peonies. Use different mediums, such as watercolors, oils, or pencil, to capture the essence and intricate details of peony flowers. Experiment with various art techniques and styles to create unique representations of peonies that reflect your artistic vision.

Peonies offer a myriad of ways to enjoy and appreciate their beauty, from cultivating them in gardens to capturing their essence through photography and artistic expression. Explore these avenues to immerse yourself in the enchanting world of peonies.

PEONY

CONCLUSION: EMBRACING THE BEAUTY OF PEONY

Peony plants (Paeonia spp.) truly embody nature's artistry and captivate our hearts with their exquisite blooms. From their vibrant colors and lush foliage to their delicate fragrance, peonies have established themselves as a beloved plant in various aspects of our lives.

Throughout history, peonies have played significant roles in cultural traditions, symbolizing beauty, prosperity, and love. They have found their place in gardens, floral arrangements, art, literature, and even medicinal practices. Today, peonies continue to enchant us, adding grace, elegance, and a touch of magic to our surroundings.

As you embark on your journey of cultivating peonies, may you find joy in witnessing their growth, from the emergence of tender shoots to the breathtaking display of blossoms. May the beauty of peonies inspire and uplift your spirit, reminding you of nature's abundant wonders.

May your gardens flourish with a colorful tapestry of peony blooms, filling the air with their sweet fragrance. May you find solace and tranquility amidst their serene presence. And may the timeless beauty of peonies bring you moments of delight, whether it's through floral arrangements, photography, art, or simply immersing yourself in their natural splendor.

WISHING YOU SUCCESSFUL CULTIVATION AND A GARDEN ADORNED WITH THE RESPLENDENT BEAUTY OF PEONIES!

PANSY

CONCLUSION: EMBRACE THE DELIGHTFUL CHARM OF PANSIES

Pansies (Viola tricolor var. hortensis) are petite flowers that carry an abundance of charm and cheerfulness. With their vibrant colors, distinctive markings, and delicate petals, they have captured the hearts of gardeners and flower enthusiasts alike.

Throughout the seasons, pansies grace our gardens, window boxes, and borders, offering a delightful display of beauty. Their resilience allows them to withstand cooler temperatures, making them an ideal choice for adding color to autumn and spring landscapes.

As you embark on the journey of cultivating pansies, may you be greeted each day with the playful smiles of these lovely flowers. May their enchanting hues brighten your outdoor spaces and bring joy to your heart. Witness their transformation from tender seedlings to a profusion of blooms, creating a tapestry of colors that enlivens any setting.

Whether you choose to adorn your flower beds, decorate your patio, or create charming floral arrangements, may pansies bring you a sense of tranquility and happiness. Their presence is a reminder to embrace the small moments of beauty in life and appreciate the simple pleasures nature provides.

WISHING YOU SUCCESSFUL CULTIVATION AND A GARDEN FILLED WITH THE DELIGHTFUL CHARM OF PANSIES!

Made in the USA
Monee, IL
01 July 2023

38328417R00056